AGES

MW01716777

Smart Alec series™

MONEY & TIME

WORD PROBLEMS

edgeucational publishing

NATIONAL STANDARDS COMPLIANT

MAKE IT FUN!

Dear Parent/Caregiver,

Make your child's learning time secure and happy by working together with your child. To help your child be successful with problem solving, be sure to have a positive attitude and make sure your child understands the problem solving strategies presented in this book!

Using objects as counters helps children understand problems. You can use beans, pennies, corn kernels, toothpicks, pebbles, or buttons to help solve the problems in the book.

Examine the problem solving below. Read these strategies with your child and use them throughout the book. Make sure your child understands how and when to use these strategies. It is important that your child develops a procedure for solving word problems. Learning how to use these strategies will give your child the tools needed for handling word problems at school and in the real world.

PROBLEM SOLVING

Solving word problems does not require a lucky guess. Use this problem solving plan as you work through this book to help you become a problem solving wiz!

1. **READ the problem carefully.** Read the problem twice! Be sure you know the meaning of the words.
2. **STATE the problem in your own words.**
3. **ASK yourself questions about the problem.** Ask: *What do I know? What do I want to find out?*
4. **DECIDE how you should solve the problem. Know your code words.** Should you use addition? Subtraction?
5. **SOLVE the problem.** Choose a method to help you solve the problems. You can draw pictures, count objects, or make a chart.
6. **CHECK the answer to see if it makes sense.**

Code Words—Certain words in a word problem will tell you if you should be adding or subtracting.

Addition Words To Know:	Subtraction Words To Know:
altogether	How many more......?
in all	difference
sum	How many......... left?
total	How many fewer.......?

This book is a companion book for the Smart Alec Series Math Computation book.

TABLE OF CONTENTS

The Amusement Park

Smart Alec and his friends are having fun at the Fun Time Amusement Park.

1 Smart Alec wants to ride on the tilt-a-whirl. He needs 3 tickets for the ride. Each ticket costs 25 cents. How much does it cost to ride the tilt-a-whirl?

75¢
____

2 After riding the tilt-a-whirl he is tired and decides to take a ride on the train. He needs 5 tickets for the ride. Each ticket costs 25 cents. How much does it cost to ride the train?

____

3 After the train ride, Smart Alec wants to ride the Ferris wheel. He looks in his pocket and finds that he has one dollar left. He knows that he needs 4 tickets for the ride and each ticket costs 25 cents. Does Smart Alec have enough money to go on the Ferris wheel?

____

The Amusement Park

Smart Alec meets his cousin on the way home from the amusement park. "Tell me all about the park," says his cousin.

Fill in the table to solve the problem.

1 "Which rides did you go on?" asks Smart Alec's cousin. Smart Alec tells his cousin about the rides. Number the rides in the order Smart Alec rode them. Look at the story on page 4 to help you solve this problem.

The Rides in the Order Smart Alec Rode Them.	Smart Alec's Rides
	Ferris wheel
	Tilt-a-whirl
	Train

2 "How much did you spend at the amusement park?" asks Smart Alec's cousin. Smart Alec begins to add up the cost of the rides. Complete the chart to help you solve the problem. How much money did he spend in all ?

____

Smart Alec's Rides	Cost of the Ride
Tilt-a-whirl	
Train	
Ferris wheel	

Count by 10

A clown is selling balloons for ten cents each. Count by tens to solve the problems.

1 Smart Alec buys 4 balloons. How much do the balloons cost in all?

40¢

2 Aleesha has 2 dollars. If she uses all of her money to buy balloons, how many balloons will she have?

______

3 Oscar wants to buy 12 balloons for Aleesha. He has one dollar. Does Oscar have enough money to buy the balloons for Aleesha?

______

Use a Picture

Smart Alec and his friends want to go to the driving range to hit golf balls. Each pail they get holds 10 golf balls.

Use the picture to solve the problems.

1 How many golf balls are in 10 pails?

100 golf balls

2 How many golf balls are in 6 pails?

________ golf balls

3 Smart Alec and Pierre get 9 pails of golf balls. How many golf balls is that altogether?

________ golf balls

4 Smart Alec got 5 pails of golf balls in the morning. He went back in the afternoon and got 3 more pails. How many golf balls did he hit altogether?

________ golf balls

Roller Coaster

Smart Alec loves to ride the Wild Mouse roller coaster. Each ride costs 20 cents.

Solve these problems.

1. On Monday, Smart Alec rides the roller coaster 2 times. How much does he spend on roller coaster rides on Monday? 40¢

2. On Tuesday, Smart Alec rides the roller coaster 3 times. How much does he spend on roller coaster rides on Tuesday? ________

3. On Saturday, Smart Alec rides the roller coaster 5 times. How much does he spend on roller coaster rides on Saturday? ________

4. How much does Smart Alec spend on roller coaster rides altogether? ________

5. Smart Alec has $3.00 to spend on roller coaster rides. How much money does he have left over after riding all the rides? ________

Roller Coaster Problems

The "Wild Mouse" roller coaster ride has 10 cars.
Each car can hold 10 people.

Solve these problems.

1 It is early in the day and the roller coaster is not busy. There are 5 roller coaster cars with 10 people in each car. How many people are riding the roller coaster?

___50___ people

2 Smart Alec likes counting the people on the roller coaster. How many people are on the roller coaster if 6 cars are filled?

________ people

3 The roller coaster is full! How many people are on the roller coaster?

________ people

4 There are 90 people in line waiting to get on the roller coaster. How many cars will they fill?

________ cars

5 Smart Alec counts 80 people on the ride. How many cars are empty?

________ cars

Count by 100!

Smart Alec and his friends stop by the fish pond to feed the fish. They buy packets of fish food. Each packet of fish food has 100 pellets inside.

Count by 100 to solve the problems.

1 If Smart Alec buys 3 packs of fish pellets, how many pellets will he be able to feed to the fish?

300 pellets

2 Aleesha buys 6 packets of fish pellets. How many fish pellets can she feed the fish?

________ pellets

3 Smart Alec picks up 8 empty bags of pellets that other people had thrown on the ground. How many fish pellets were in those 8 bags before they were empty?

________ pellets

The Arcade

Smart Alec and his friends like to play skee ball in the arcade.

Look at the skee ball game below and solve the problems.

1 Smart Alec rolls 3 skee balls. The balls land on 100, 300, and 400. How many points does Smart Alec get altogether?

800 points

2 Oscar has 600 points. How many more points does he need to get 1000 points?

________ more points

3 Aleesha's first ball landed on 500! She rolls another ball and it lands on 200. Which number does Aleesha need to reach 1000 points?

____

Use a Graph

Smart Alec buys a sheet of tickets to ride some rides at the Amusement Park. Each ticket costs 10 cents.

Use the information from the table below to solve the problems.

Rides	Tickets needed for rides
Tilt-a-Whirl	
Wild Mouse Roller Coaster	
Bumper Cars	
Spinning Teacups	

1 Aleesha wants to ride on the Spinning Teacups. How many tickets does she need ? ___3___ tickets

How much does the ride cost? ___30¢___

2 Smart Alec wants to ride the Wild Mouse roller coaster. How many tickets does he need? ________ tickets

How much does the ride cost? ________

3 Oscar likes to ride the Tilt-a-Whirl. How many tickets does he need to ride it twice? ________ tickets

How much does he pay to ride the Tilt-a-Whirl? ________

4 Oscar and Aleesha want to ride the Bumper Cars together. How many tickets in all do they give to the cashier to ride the cars?

________ tickets

In the Arcade!

Smart Alec and his friends are excited about playing the Ring Toss game.

Look at the pictures to solve the problems about place value.

Hundreds	Tens	Ones
5	0	0

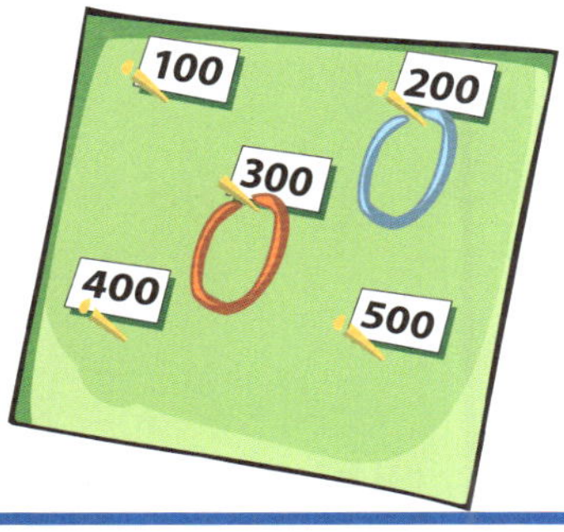

How many points altogether? 500

How many hundreds? 5

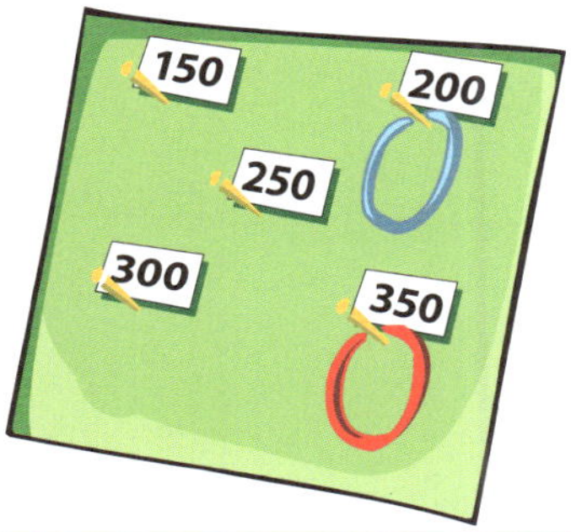

How many points altogether? ________

How many hundreds? ________

How many tens? ________

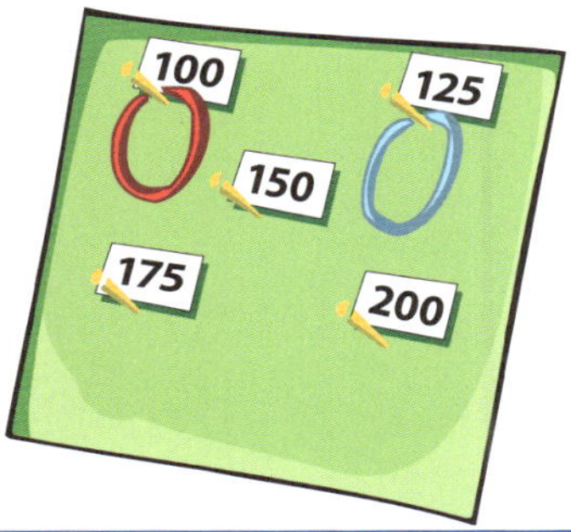

How many points altogether? ________

How many hundreds? ________

How many tens? ________

How many ones? ________

The Buses

Use the information in these problems to help Smart Alec find the answers!

1 Buses at the Fun Time Amusement Park are lined up 10 in a row. There are 50 buses parked at 9 A.M. How many rows of buses are there? ___5___ rows

2 At 12 P.M. there are 10 rows of buses in the parking lot. How many buses is that? ________ buses

3 There are 85 buses in the lot at 2 P.M. How many rows are needed to park all of the buses? ________ rows

4 There are 325 buses in the lot at 3 P.M. Write 325 in the chart below.

	Place Value		Number
How many hundreds?	3	=	300
How many tens?	________	=	________
How many ones?	________	=	________

Complete the Chart

The hot dog man is counting his money and needs to separate it into ones, tens and hundred dollar bills.

Use the chart below to help him sort his money.

Time	Money Counted
11 A.M.	$251
1 P.M.	$349
2 P.M.	$462
4 P.M.	$578
6 P.M.	$862

Complete this chart using the information from the chart above.

Time	How Many Hundreds?	How Many Tens?	How Many Ones?
11 A.M.	2	5	1
1 P.M.			
2 P.M.			
4 P.M.			
6 P.M.			

What's the Number?

Solve these problems using the digits and the clues. Use each digit once to make a number. Use 2, 4, and 5.

Hundreds	Tens	Ones
4	5	2

1 My number is more than 300.
The 10's place is worth 50.

My number is 452.

My other number is even.
It's less than 300.

My number is ________.

Use 0, 4, and 7

2 My number is more than 600.
The 10's place is worth 40.

My number is ________.

My other number is odd.
It's more than 300.

My number is ________.

Use 1, 4, and 9

3 My number is more than 300.
The 10's place is worth more than 50.

My number is ________.

My other number is even.
It's more than 500.

My number is ________.

Count Tickets

At the end of the day the cashier needs to count all the left over tickets and bundle them up into hundreds, tens, and ones.

Solve these problems.

1 The cashier has 553 tickets. If she puts them into groups of 100, how many full groups of 100 does she have?

___5___ groups of 100

How many groups of 10 tickets does she have left over?

___5___ groups of 10

How many single tickets (ones) does she have left over?

___3___ single tickets left over

2 Later in the evening, the cashier found 372 more tickets. How many full groups of 100 can she make using these tickets?

________ groups of 100

How many groups of 10 does she have left over?

________ groups of 10

How many single tickets (ones) does she have left over?

________ single tickets left over

Read and Think!

Solve these problems.

1 There are 10 fish jumping in the pond. Three fish jump on one side. How many fish jump on the other side of the pond?

10 – 3 = 7 fish or 10 – 7 = 3

2 Smart Alec has 8 bags of fish pellets. He has 3 left after he gives Oscar some. How many bags of fish pellets does he give to Oscar?

8 – _____ = 3 or 8 – 3 = _____

3 Aleesha knocks down 6 bears in a game on her second try. She knocks down 11 bears altogether. How many bears did she knock down on her first try?

11 – _____ = 6 or 11 – 6 = _____

4 In the morning Smart Alec rides the Whip 4 times. By the end of the afternoon, he has ridden it 12 times. How many times does he ride it in the afternoon?

12 – 4 = _____ or 12 – _____ = 4

Addition and Subtraction

Review the code words on page 2. Solve these story problems using addition or subtraction. Underline the code words which tell you to add or subtract.

1 Smart Alec has 12 tickets. He gives Aleesha 10. How many tickets does Smart Alec have left?

__12__ __-__ __10__ = __2__ tickets

2 There are 11 fish in the pond. 10 fish jump out to catch some fish pellets. How many are left in the water?

______ ____ ______ = ______ left

3 Aleesha needs to knock down 8 bears in a game to win a prize. She already knocked down 7 of them. How many more bears does she need to knock down?

______ ____ ______ = ______ more

4 Smart Alec rides the Wild Mouse 8 times. Aleesha rides it 2 times. How many times do they ride the Wild Mouse in all?

______ ____ ______ = ______ times

Use Addition

Solve the problems and underline the code words.

1 Smart Alec knocks down 5 bears. Oscar knocks down 6 bears. How many bears do they knock down in all?

5 + 6 = 11 bears

2 Aleesha rides the Wild Mouse 7 times. Smart Alec rides it 9 times. How many times do they ride it altogether?

________ + ________ = ________ times

3 Eight buses pull into Fun Park. Seven more buses follow. How many buses pull into the park altogether?

________ + ________ = ________ buses

4 Oscar and Aleesha each eat 7 hot dogs. How many hot dogs do they eat in all?

________ + ________ = ________ hot dogs

5 Ten fish jump up out of the water to be fed. Then, seven more jump up. How many fish altogether jump up to be fed?

________ + ________ = ________ fish

Use Addition

Solve the problems and underline the code words.

1 In the pond there are 6 ducks and 8 swans. <u>How many</u> ducks and swans are there <u>in all</u>?

6 + 8 = 14 altogether

2 Smart Alec wins 8 large prizes and 9 small prizes. What is the sum of the prizes he wins?

________ + ________ = ________ prizes

3 Smart Alec eats 9 chocolate chip cookies and Oscar eats 6 chocolate chip cookies. How many chocolate chip cookies do they eat in all?

________ + ________ = ________ cookies

4 Oscar and Aleesha share fried onion rings. Aleesha eats 9 and Oscar eats 10. Find the total number of onion rings they eat.

________ + ________ = ________ onion rings

Keep on Adding!

Circle pairs of numbers that add up to a sum equal to, or greater than, 13. The numbers must be next to each other. How many can you find?

6	4	2	9	1	8	2	7
3	5	8	3	7	6	5	9
4	7	9	2	5	3	4	1
2	6	4	5	2	6	3	8
7	5	3	9	6	7	2	4
6	2	5	7	3	8	4	5

Use a Clock

Solve the addition problems. Show the correct time on the clocks.

1 Smart Alec leaves for Fun Time Amusement Park at 8:00 a.m. It takes him 2 hours to get there. What time does he arrive at the Park?

10:00 o'clock

2 Smart Alec waits in line to get tickets for some rides. He stands in line at 11:00 a.m. It takes 1 hour to get to the front of the line. What time does Smart Alec get his tickets?

_______ o'clock

3 Fun Time Amusement Park opens at 10:00 a.m. Smart Alec is there for 5 hours. What time does Smart Alec leave the park?

_______ o'clock

Keep on Adding!

Circle any set of numbers that add up to a sum equal to or greater than 20. Circle the numbers in any direction. The numbers must go in a straight line. Do not use a number more than once. How many sets can you find?

6	4	2	9	1	8	2	7
3	5	8	3	7	6	5	9
4	7	9	2	5	3	4	1
2	6	4	5	2	6	3	8
7	5	3	9	6	7	2	4
6	2	5	7	3	8	4	5

Keep on Adding!

Circle any two or three numbers that add up to a <u>sum equal to or greater than 12.</u> Circle the numbers in any direction. The numbers must be in a straight line. *How many sets can you find?

6	4	2	9	1	8	2	7
3	5	8	3	7	6	5	9
4	7	9	2	5	3	4	1
2	6	4	5	2	6	3	8
7	5	3	9	6	7	2	4
6	2	5	7	3	8	4	5

*do not use a number more than once.

Draw Pictures

Draw pictures to help you solve the problems.
Then, use subtraction to write a number sentence.

1 Smart Alec sees 11 ducks on the the pond. 5 ducks fly away. How many ducks are left swimming?

Draw a picture of your problem.

Number sentence: ___11___ − ___5___ = ___6___

2 Twelve people are waiting to ride the Wild Mouse. Eight people get on the ride. How many people are left waiting?

Draw a picture of your problem.

Number sentence: ________ − ________ = ________

Ask Questions

Another problem solving strategy:

Learn to ask yourself these questions:

What do I know?

What do I want to find out?

Use this strategy to solve the problem.

1 There are 14 cars on the Teacup Ride.
8 of them are full. How many cars are empty?

What do I know?

I know there are 14 cars on the Teacup Ride.

I know that 8 of the cars are full.

What do I want to find out?

I want to find out how many cars are empty.

I know I will have less than 14 cars, so I must subtract.

14 – 8 = 6 cars

2 Smart Alec has 15 balls to throw at the ball toss game.
He uses 9 of them. How many balls are left to throw?

What do I know? ____________________

What do I want to find out? ____________________

______ – ______ = ______ balls left

Asking Questions

Ask questions to solve problems.

1 Smart Alec buys 13 packets of fish pellets. He gives Oscar 9 of them. How many packets does Smart Alec have left?

What do I know? ______________________

What do I want to find out? ______________________

_______ – _______ = _______ packets left

2 Oscar has 19 tickets. He uses 9 of the tickets to buy a hot dog and soda. How many tickets does he have left?

What do I know? ______________________

What do I want to find out? ______________________

_______ – _______ = _______ tickets

Use Subtraction

Remember to think about what you know and what you want to find out. Also, look for code words.

Write number sentences to solve the problems.

1 Smart Alec rides the Ferris Wheel 15 times. Aleesha rides the Ferris Wheel 6 times. How many fewer times does Aleesha ride the Ferris Wheel than Smart Alec?

15 – 6 = 9 fewer times

2 There are 11 hot dogs on the table. Smart Alec and his friends eat 6 of them. How many are left on the table?

________ – ________ = ________ left

3 There are 12 pizzas in the oven. Five of them have pepperoni. The rest have extra cheese. How many have extra cheese?

________ – ________ = ________ extra cheese

4 There are 13 different kinds of ice cream. 6 kinds of ice cream have nuts. How many kinds of ice cream do not have nuts?

________ – ________ = ________ no nuts

Keep Subtracting!

Write number sentences to solve the problems.

1 While Smart Alec hits golf balls at the driving range, 17 of the golf balls roll onto the grass. He finds 7 of them. How many golf balls are lost?

17 – 7 = 10 balls lost

2 There are 18 bears to knock down at the ball toss booth. Oscar knocks down 9 of them. How many are left to knock down?

________ – ________ = ________ left

3 Oscar needs 18 tickets to go into the Fun House. He only has 8. How many more tickets does he need to go into the Fun House?

________ – ________ = ________ more tickets

4 Eleven people are in line to ride the Whip. Only 8 people get on the ride. How many people are still waiting?

________ – ________ = ________ people

Subtraction Problems

Solve these subtraction problems. Check each problem by creating an addition problem to prove your answer.

1 Smart Alec wins 16 small prizes at the Amusement Park. His friends win 8 prizes. How many more prizes does Smart Alec win than his friends?

Subtraction Problem:

16 − 8 = 8 prizes

Addition Check Problem:

8 + 8 = 16 prizes

2 There are 15 rides at Fun Park. Oscar is too big to go on 5 of the rides. How many rides is Oscar able to go on?

Subtraction Problem:

______ − ______ = ______ rides

Addition Check Problem:

______ + ______ = ______ rides

Subtraction Problems

Solve these subtraction problems. Check each problem by creating an addition problem to prove your answer.

1 A clown carries 16 balloons. Nine of the balloons blow away. How many balloons does he have left?

Subtraction Problem:

________ − ________ = ________ balloons

Addition Check Problem:

________ + ________ = ________ balloons

2 The hot dog man has 17 hot dogs. Some have pickles on them. Nine of the hot dogs have mustard on them. How many hot dogs have pickles on them?

Subtraction Problem:

________ − ________ = ________ hot dogs

Addition Check Problem:

________ + ________ = ________ hot dogs

Tic-Tac-Toe math

Solve each problem. For each puzzle find the three problems in a straight line that have the same answer. Draw a line through the answer.

1

8 − 4 = 4	10 − 6 = 4	12 − 6 = 6
10 − 2 = 8	12 − 8 = 4	11 − 5 = 6
9 − 5 = 4	10 − 3 = 7	11 − 7 = 4

2

17 − 8 = 9	12 − 9 = 3	11 − 5 = 6
15 − 9 = 6	14 − 8 = 6	13 − 7 = 6
13 − 8 = 5	16 − 8 = 8	11 − 4 = 7

Word Problems

Decide what operation (+ or −) you will use to solve each problem. Then, make a number sentence and solve each problem.

1 Oscar and Aleesha wait under a tree for Smart Alec to get his ticket and take a ride on the Wild Mouse. Smart Alec waits 20 minutes to get his ticket. The ride lasted 12 minutes. How many minutes did Oscar and Aleesha wait for Smart Alec?

20 + 12 = 32 minutes

2 Oscar's score at the skee ball game was 650. Smart Alec's score is 400. How many more points does Oscar have than Smart Alec?

650 − 400 = 250 more points

3 Smart Alec's friend is 52 inches tall. Aleesha's friend is 31 inches tall. How many inches taller is Smart Alec's friend than Aleesha's friend?

52 − 31 = 21 inches taller

4 Smart Alec buys a hot dog for $2.50. He also pays $1.00 for a can of lemonade. How much money does he spend altogether?

$1.00 + $2.50 = $3.50

Word Problems

Use problem solving strategies to solve these problems.

1 The hot dog man sells 255 hot dogs by noon. At 3:00 he has sold 424 more. How many hot dogs does he sell altogether by 3:00?

255 + 424 = 679 hot dogs

2 Smart Alec needs to knock down 35 bears at the ball toss booth to get a prize. He already knocked down 17. How many more bears does he need to knock down?

35 − 17 = 18 more bears

3 There are 156 people in line waiting to get into Fun Time Amusement Park. 123 more people get in line. How many people are in line altogether?

156 + 123 = 279 people

4 Smart Alec has 26 tickets left at the end of the day. Oscar has 11 tickets left. How many tickets do they have between them? How many more tickets does Smart Alec have than Oscar?

26 + 11 = 37 tickets altogether

26 − 11 = 15 more tickets

Number Square Addition

The numbers in each row across total the numbers to the right of each row. The numbers in each column total the numbers at the bottom of each column.

Use numbers between 1 and 9 to fill in the spaces in the grid.

8	2	8	6	24
8	6			32
1	7	7	3	18
7		6	9	29
24	22	30	27	

Challenge Your Thinking

The numbers in each row across total the numbers to the right of each row. The numbers in each column total the numbers at the bottom of each column.

Use numbers between 1 and 9 to fill in the spaces in the grid.

9	5	6	4	24
1	6		5	19
5		8	2	17
3	7		3	15
18	20	23	14	

Challenge Your Thinking

The numbers in each row across total the numbers to the right of each row. The numbers in each column total the numbers at the bottom of each column.

Use numbers between 1 and 10 to fill in the spaces in the grid.

5	7	5	6	23
5	6	10		29
	5	9	4	26
	7		7	25
21	25	32	25	

Challenge Your Thinking

The numbers in each row across total the numbers to the right of each row. The numbers in each column total the numbers at the bottom of each column.

Use numbers between 1 and 9 to fill in the spaces in the grid.

9		4	3	24
2	5	6	8	21
	2	3		17
4		1	3	16
20	23	14	21	

Answer Key

The Amusement Park

Smart Alec and his friends are having fun at the Fun Time Amusement Park.

1 Smart Alec wants to ride on the tilt-a-whirl. He needs 3 tickets for the ride. Each ticket costs 25 cents. How much does it cost to ride the tilt-a-whirl?

75¢

2 After riding the tilt-a-whirl he is tired and decides to take a ride on the train. He needs 5 tickets for the ride. Each ticket costs 25 cents. How much does it cost to ride the train?

$1.25

3 After the train ride, Smart Alec wants to ride the Ferris wheel. He looks in his pocket and finds that he had one dollar left. He knows that he needs 4 tickets for the ride and each ticket costs 25 cents. Does Smart Alec have enough money to go on the Ferris wheel?

Yes

The Amusement Park

Smart Alec meets his cousin on the way home from the amusement park. "Tell me all about the park," says his cousin.

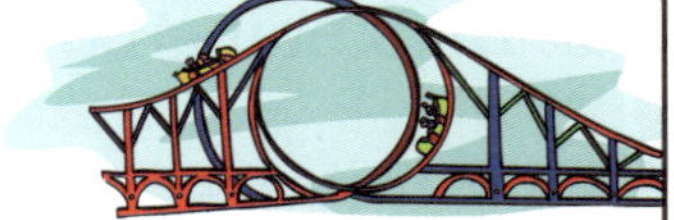

Fill in the table to solve the problem.

1 "Which rides did you go on?" asks Smart Alec's cousin. Smart Alec tells his cousin about the rides. Number the rides in the order Smart Alec rode them. Look at the story on page 4 to help you solve this problem.

The Rides in the Order Smart Alec Rode Them.	Smart Alec's Rides
3rd	Ferris wheel
1st	Tilt-a-whirl
2nd	Train

2 "How much did you spend at the amusement park?" asks Smart Alec's cousin. Smart Alec begins to add up the cost of the rides. Complete the chart to help you solve the problem. How much money did he spend in all ?

$3.00

Smart Alec's Rides	Cost of the Ride
Tilt-a-whirl	75¢
Train	$1.25
Ferris wheel	$1.00

Count by 10

A clown is selling balloons for ten cents each. Count by tens to solve the problems.

1 Smart Alec buys 4 balloons. How much do the balloons cost in all?

40¢

2 Aleesha has 2 dollars. If she uses all of her money to buy balloons, how many balloons will she have?

20

3 Oscar wants to buy 12 balloons for Aleesha. He has one dollar. Does Oscar have enough money to buy the balloons for Aleesha?

No

Use a Picture

Smart Alec and his friends want to go to the driving range to hit golf balls. Each pail they get holds 10 golf balls.

Use the picture to solve the problems.

1 How many golf balls are in 10 pails?

100 golf balls

2 How many golf balls are in 6 pails?

60 golf balls

3 Smart Alec and Pierre get 9 pails of golf balls. How many golf balls is that altogether?

90 golf balls

4 Smart Alec got 5 pails of golf balls in the morning. He went back in the afternoon and got 3 more pails. How many golf balls did he hit altogether?

80 golf balls

Roller Coaster

Smart Alec loves to ride the Wild Mouse roller coaster. Each ride costs 20 cents.

Solve these problems.

1. On Monday, Smart Alec rides the roller coaster 2 times. How much does he spend on roller coaster rides on Monday? 40¢

2. On Tuesday, Smart Alec rides the roller coaster 3 times. How much does he spend on roller coaster rides on Tuesday? 60¢

3. On Saturday, Smart Alec rides the roller coaster 5 times. How much does he spend on roller coaster rides on Saturday? $1.00

4. How much does Smart Alec spend on roller coaster rides altogether? $2.00

5. Smart Alec has $3.00 to spend on roller coaster rides. How much money does he have left over after riding all the rides? $1.00

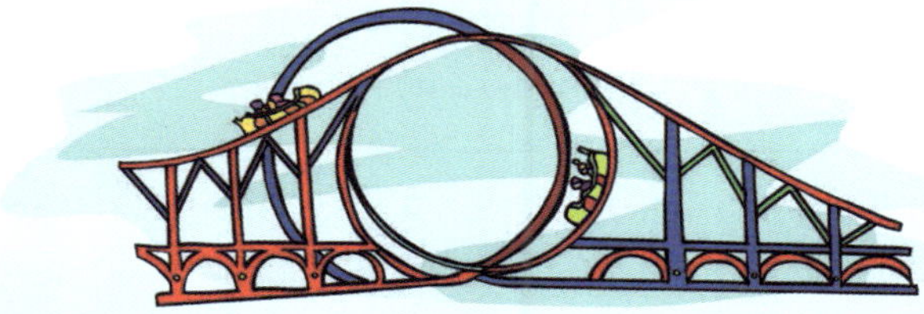

Roller Coaster Problems

The "Wild Mouse" roller coaster ride has 10 cars. Each car can hold 10 people.

Solve these problems.

1. It is early in the day and the roller coaster is not busy. There are 5 roller coaster cars with 10 people in each car. How many people are riding the roller coaster?
   50 people

2. Smart Alec likes counting the people on the roller coaster. How many people are on the roller coaster if 6 cars are filled?
   60 people

3. The roller coaster is full! How many people are on the roller coaster?
   100 people

4. There are 90 people in line waiting to get on the roller coaster. How many cars will they fill?
   9 cars

5. Smart Alec counts 80 people on the ride. How many cars are empty?
   2 cars

Count by 100!

Smart Alec and his friends stop by the fish pond to feed the fish. They buy packets of fish food. Each packet of fish food has 100 pellets inside.

Count by 100 to solve the problems.

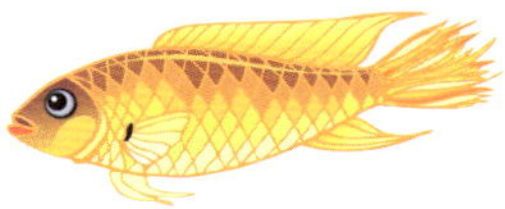

1. If Smart Alec buys 3 packs of fish pellets, how many pellets will he be able to feed to the fish?
   300 pellets

2. Aleesha buys 6 packets of fish pellets. How many fish pellets can she feed the fish?
   600 pellets

3. Smart Alec picks up 8 empty bags of pellets that other people had thrown on the ground. How many fish pellets were in those 8 bags before they were empty?
   800 pellets

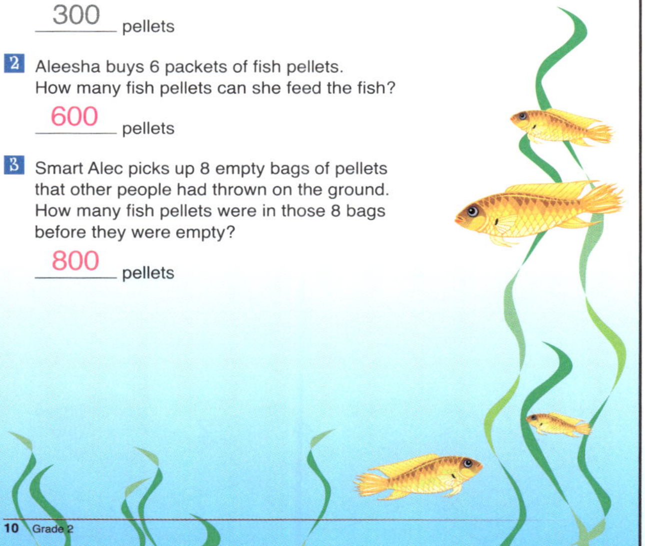

The Arcade

Smart Alec and his friends like to play skee ball in the arcade.

Look at the skee ball game below and solve the problems.

1. Smart Alec rolls 3 skee balls. The balls land on 100, 300, and 400. How many points does Smart Alec get altogether?
   800 points

2. Oscar has 600 points. How many more points does he need to get 1000 points?
   400 more points

3. Aleesha's first ball landed on 500! She rolls another ball and it lands on 200. Which number does Aleesha need to reach 1000 points?
   300

Use a Graph

Smart Alec buys a sheet of tickets to ride some rides at the Amusement Park. Each ticket costs 10 cents.

Use the information from the table below to solve the problems.

Rides	Tickets needed for rides
Tilt-a-Whirl	
Wild Mouse Roller Coaster	
Bumper Cars	
Spinning Teacups	

1 Aleesha wants to ride on the Spinning Teacups. How many tickets does she need ? 3 tickets

How much does the ride cost? 30¢

2 Smart Alec wants to ride the Wild Mouse roller coaster. How many tickets does he need? 5 tickets

How much does the ride cost? 50¢

3 Oscar likes to ride the Tilt-a-Whirl. How many tickets does he need to ride it twice? 8 tickets

How much does he pay to ride the Tilt-a-Whirl? 80¢

4 Oscar and Aleesha want to ride the Bumper Cars together. How many tickets in all do they give to the cashier to ride the cars?

4 tickets

In the Arcade!

Smart Alec and his friends are excited about playing the Ring Toss game.

Look at the pictures to solve the problems about place value.

Hundreds	Tens	Ones
5	0	0

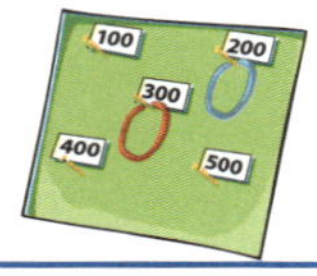	How many points altogether? 500 How many hundreds? 5
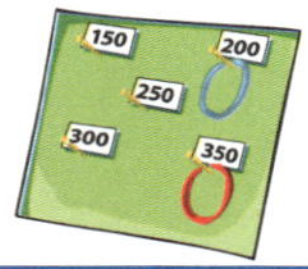	How many points altogether? 550 How many hundreds? 5 How many tens? 5
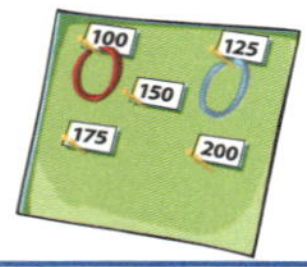	How many points altogether? 225 How many hundreds? 2 How many tens? 2 How many ones? 5

The Buses

Use the information in these problems to help Smart Alec find the answers!

1 Buses at the Fun Time Amusement Park are lined up 10 in a row. There are 50 buses parked at 9 A.M. How many rows of buses are there? 5 rows

2 At 12 P.M. there are 10 rows of buses in the parking lot. How many buses is that? 100 buses

3 There are 85 buses in the lot at 2 P.M. How many rows are needed to park all of the buses? 9 rows

4 There are 325 buses in the lot at 3 P.M. Write 325 in the chart below.

	Place Value		Number
How many hundreds?	3	=	300
How many tens?	2	=	20
How many ones?	5	=	5

Complete the Chart

The hot dog man is counting his money and needs to separate it into ones, tens and hundred dollar bills.

Use the chart below to help him sort his money.

Time	Money Counted
11 A.M.	$251
1 P.M.	$349
2 P.M.	$462
4 P.M.	$578
6 P.M.	$862

Complete this chart using the information from the chart above.

Time	How Many Hundreds?	How Many Tens?	How Many Ones?
11 A.M.	2	5	1
1 P.M.	3	4	9
2 P.M.	4	6	2
4 P.M.	5	7	8
6 P.M.	8	6	2

What's the Number?

Solve these problems using the digits and the clues. Use each digit once to make a number. Use 2, 4, and 5.

Hundreds	Tens	Ones
4	5	2

1 My number is more than 300. The 10's place is worth 50.

My number is 452.

My other number is even. It's less than 300.

My number is 254.

Use 0, 4, and 7

2 My number is more than 600. The 10's place is worth 40.

My number is 740.

My other number is odd. It's more than 300.

My number is 407.

Use 1, 4, and 9

3 My number is more than 300. The 10's place is worth more than 50.

My number is 491.

My other number is even. It's more than 500.

My number is 914.

Count Tickets

At the end of the day the cashier needs to count all the left over tickets and bundle them up into hundreds, tens, and ones.

Solve these problems.

1 The cashier has 553 tickets. If she puts them into groups of 100, how many full groups of 100 does she have?

5 groups of 100

How many groups of 10 tickets does she have left over?

5 groups of 10

How many single tickets (ones) does she have left over?

3 single tickets left over

2 Later in the evening, the cashier found 372 more tickets. How many full groups of 100 can she make using these tickets?

3 groups of 100

How many groups of 10 does she have left over?

7 groups of 10

How many single tickets (ones) does she have left over?

2 single tickets left over

Read and Think!

Solve these problems.

1 There are 10 fish jumping in the pond. Three fish jump on one side. How many fish jump on the other side of the pond?

10 – 3 = 7 fish or 10 – 7 = 3

2 Smart Alec has 8 bags of fish pellets. He has 3 left after he gives Oscar some. How many bags of fish pellets does he give to Oscar?

8 – 5 = 3 or 8 – 3 = 5

3 Aleesha knocks down 6 bears in a game on her second try. She knocks down 11 bears altogether. How many bears did she knock down on her first try?

11 – 5 = 6 or 11 – 6 = 5

4 In the morning Smart Alec rides the Whip 4 times. By the end of the afternoon, he has ridden it 12 times. How many times does he ride it in the afternoon?

12 – 4 = 8 or 12 – 8 = 4

Addition and Subtraction

Review the code words on page 2. Solve these story problems using addition or subtraction. Underline the code words which tell you to add or subtract.

1 Smart Alec has 12 tickets. He gives Aleesha 10. How many tickets does Smart Alec have left?

12 - 10 = 2 tickets

2 There are 11 fish in the pond. 10 fish jump out to catch some fish pellets. How many are left in the water?

11 - 10 = 1 left

3 Aleesha needs to knock down 8 bears in a game to win a prize. She already knocked down 7 of them. How many more bears does she need to knock down?

8 - 7 = 1 more

4 Smart Alec rides the Wild Mouse 8 times. Aleesha rides it 2 times. How many times do they ride the Wild Mouse in all?

8 + 2 = 10 times

Use Addition

Solve the problems and underline the code words.

1 Smart Alec knocks down 5 bears. Oscar knocks down 6 bears. How many bears do they knock down in all?

5 + 6 = 11 bears

2 Aleesha rides the Wild Mouse 7 times. Smart Alec rides it 9 times. How many times do they ride it altogether?

9 + 7 = 16 times

3 Eight buses pull into Fun Park. Seven more buses follow. How many buses pull into the park altogether?

8 + 7 = 15 buses

4 Oscar and Aleesha each eat 7 hot dogs. How many hot dogs do they eat in all?

7 + 7 = 14 hot dogs

5 Ten fish jump up out of the water to be fed. Then, seven more jump up. How many fish altogether jump up to be fed?

10 + 7 = 17 fish

Use Addition

Solve the problems and underline the code words.

1 In the pond there are 6 ducks and 8 swans. How many ducks and swans are there in all?

6 + 8 = 14 altogether

2 Smart Alec wins 8 large prizes and 9 small prizes. What is the sum of the prizes he wins?

8 + 9 = 17 prizes

3 Smart Alec eats 9 chocolate chip cookies and Oscar eats 6 chocolate chip cookies. How many chocolate chip cookies do they eat in all?

9 + 6 = 15 cookies

4 Oscar and Aleesha share fried onion rings. Aleesha eats 9 and Oscar eats 10. Find the total number of onion rings they eat.

9 + 10 = 19 onion rings

Keep on Adding!

Circle pairs of numbers that add up to a sum equal to, or greater than, 13. The numbers must be next to each other. How many can you find?

6	4	2	9	1	8	2	7
3	5	8	3	7	6	5	9
4	7	9	2	5	3	4	1
2	6	4	5	2	6	3	8
7	5	3	9	6	7	2	4
6	2	5	7	3	8	4	5

Use a Clock

Solve the addition problems. Show the correct time on the clocks.

1 Smart Alec leaves for Fun Time Amusement Park at 8:00 a.m. It takes him 2 hours to get there. What time does he arrive at the Park?

10:00 o'clock

2 Smart Alec waits in line to get tickets for some rides. He stands in line at 11:00 a.m. It takes 1 hour to get to the front of the line. What time does Smart Alec get his tickets?

12:00 o'clock

3 Fun Time Amusement Park opens at 10:00 a.m. Smart Alec is there for 5 hours. What time does Smart Alec leave the park?

3:00 o'clock

Keep on Adding!

Circle any set of numbers that add up to a <u>sum equal to or greater than 20.</u> Circle the numbers in any direction. The numbers must go in a straight line. Do not use a number more than once. How many sets can you find?

6	4	2	9	1	8	2	7
3	5	8	3	7	6	5	9
4	7	9	2	5	3	4	1
2	6	4	5	2	6	3	8
7	5	3	9	6	7	2	4
6	2	5	7	3	8	4	5

Keep on Adding!

Circle any two or three numbers that add up to a <u>sum equal to or greater than 12.</u> Circle the numbers in any direction. The numbers must be in a straight line. *How many sets can you find?

6	4	2	9	1	8	2	7
3	5	8	3	7	6	5	9
4	7	9	2	5	3	4	1
2	6	4	5	2	6	3	8
7	5	3	9	6	7	2	4
6	2	5	7	3	8	4	5

*do not use a number more than once.

Draw Pictures

Draw pictures to help you solve the problems. Then, use subtraction to write a number sentence.

1 Smart Alec sees 11 ducks on the the pond. 5 ducks fly away. How many ducks are left swimming?

Draw a picture of your problem.

Number sentence: 11 – 5 = 6

2 Twelve people are waiting to ride the Wild Mouse. Eight people get on the ride. How many people are left waiting?

Draw a picture of your problem.

Number sentence: 12 – 8 = 4

Ask Questions

Another problem solving strategy:

Learn to ask yourself these questions:

What do I know?

What do I want to find out?

Use this strategy to solve the problem.

1 There are 14 cars on the Teacup Ride. 8 of them are full. How many cars are empty?

What do I know?

I know there are 14 cars on the Teacup Ride.

I know that 8 of the cars are full.

What do I want to find out?

I want to find out how many cars are empty.

I know I will have less than 14 cars, so I must subtract.

14 – 8 = 6 cars

2 Smart Alec has 15 balls to throw at the ball toss game. He uses 9 of them. How many balls are left to throw?

What do I know? How many balls Smart Alec had, and how many he used

What do I want to find out? How many balls Smart Alec has left

15 – 9 = 6 balls left

Asking Questions

Ask questions to solve problems.

1. Smart Alec buys 13 packets of fish pellets. He gives Oscar 9 of them. How many packets does Smart Alec have left?

   What do I know? He bought 13 packets and gave 9 of them away.

   What do I want to find out? How many packets he has left

   13 – 9 = 4 packets left

2. Oscar has 19 tickets. He uses 9 of the tickets to buy a hot dog and soda. How many tickets does he have left?

   What do I know? He had 19 tickets and used 9 of them.

   What do I want to find out? How many tickets are left

   19 – 9 = 10 tickets

Use Subtraction

Remember to think about what you know and what you want to find out. Also, look for code words.

Write number sentences to solve the problems.

1. Smart Alec rides the Ferris Wheel 15 times. Aleesha rides the Ferris Wheel 6 times. How many fewer times does Aleesha ride the Ferris Wheel than Smart Alec?

   15 – 6 = 9 fewer times

2. There are 11 hot dogs on the table. Smart Alec and his friends eat 6 of them. How many are left on the table?

   11 – 6 = 5 left

3. There are 12 pizzas in the oven. Five of them have pepperoni. The rest have extra cheese. How many have extra cheese?

   12 – 5 = 7 extra cheese

4. There are 13 different kinds of ice cream. 6 kinds of ice cream have nuts. How many kinds of ice cream do not have nuts?

   13 – 6 = 7 no nuts

Keep Subtracting!

Write number sentences to solve the problems.

1. While Smart Alec hits golf balls at the driving range, 17 of the golf balls roll onto the grass. He finds 7 of them. How many golf balls are lost?

   17 – 7 = 10 balls lost

2. There are 18 bears to knock down at the ball toss booth. Oscar knocks down 9 of them. How many are left to knock down?

   18 – 9 = 9 left

3. Oscar needs 18 tickets to go into the Fun House. He only has 8. How many more tickets does he need to go into the Fun House?

   18 – 8 = 10 more tickets

4. Eleven people are in line to ride the Whip. Only 8 people get on the ride. How many people are still waiting?

   11 – 8 = 3 people

Subtraction Problems

Solve these subtraction problems. Check each problem by creating an addition problem to prove your answer.

1. Smart Alec wins 16 small prizes at the Amusement Park. His friends win 8 prizes. How many more prizes does Smart Alec win than his friends?

   Subtraction Problem:

   16 – 8 = 8 prizes

   Addition Check Problem:

   8 + 8 = 16 prizes

2. There are 15 rides at Fun Park. Oscar is too big to go on 5 of the rides. How many rides is Oscar able to go on?

   Subtraction Problem:

   15 – 5 = 10 rides

   Addition Check Problem:

   10 + 5 = 15 rides

Subtraction Problems

Solve these subtraction problems. Check each problem by creating an addition problem to prove your answer.

1 A clown carries 16 balloons. Nine of the balloons blow away. How many balloons does he have left?

Subtraction Problem:

16 – 9 = 7 balloons

Addition Check Problem:

9 + 7 = 16 balloons

2 The hot dog man has 17 hot dogs. Some have pickles on them. Nine of the hot dogs have mustard on them. How many hot dogs have pickles on them?

Subtraction Problem:

17 – 9 = 8 hot dogs

Addition Check Problem:

9 + 8 = 17 hot dogs

Tic-Tac-Toe math

Solve each problem. For each puzzle find the three problems in a straight line that have the same answer. Draw a line through the answer.

1

8 – 4 = 4	10 – 6 = 4	12 – 6 = 6
10 – 2 = 8	12 – 8 = 4	11 – 5 = 6
9 – 5 = 4	10 – 3 = 7	11 – 7 = 4

2

17 – 8 = 9	12 – 9 = 3	11 – 5 = 6
15 – 9 = 6	14 – 8 = 6	13 – 7 = 6
13 – 8 = 5	16 – 8 = 8	11 – 4 = 7

Word Problems

Decide what operation (+ or –) you will use to solve each problem. Then, make a number sentence and solve each problem.

1 Oscar and Aleesha wait under a tree for Smart Alec to get his ticket and take a ride on the Wild Mouse. Smart Alec waits 20 minutes to get his ticket. The ride lasted 12 minutes. How many minutes did Oscar and Aleesha wait for Smart Alec?

20 + 12 = 32 minutes

2 Oscar's score at the skee ball game was 650. Smart Alec's score is 400. How many more points does Oscar have than Smart Alec?

650 - 400 = 250 more points

3 Smart Alec's friend is 52 inches tall. Aleesha's friend is 31 inches tall. How many inches taller is Smart Alec's friend than Aleesha's friend?

52 - 31 = 21 inches taller

4 Smart Alec buys a hot dog for $2.50. He also pays $1.00 for a can of lemonade. How much money does he spend altogether?

$ 2.50 + $ 1.00 = $ 3.50

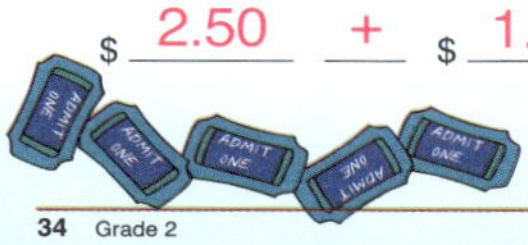

Word Problems

Use problem solving strategies to solve these problems.

1 The hot dog man sells 255 hot dogs by noon. At 3:00 he has sold 424 more. How many hot dogs does he sell altogether by 3:00?

255 + 424 = 679 hot dogs

2 Smart Alec needs to knock down 35 bears at the ball toss booth to get a prize. He already knocked down 17. How many more bears does he need to knock down?

35 - 17 = 18 more bears

3 There are 156 people in line waiting to get into Fun Time Amusement Park. 123 more people get in line. How many people are in line altogether?

156 + 123 = 279 people

4 Smart Alec has 26 tickets left at the end of the day. Oscar has 11 tickets left. How many tickets do they have between them? How many more tickets does Smart Alec have than Oscar?

26 + 11 = 37 tickets altogether

26 - 11 = 15 more tickets

Number Square Addition

The numbers in each row across total the numbers to the right of each row. The numbers in each column total the numbers at the bottom of each column.

Use numbers between 1 and 9 to fill in the spaces in the grid.

8	2	8	6	24
8	6	9	9	32
1	7	7	3	18
7	7	6	9	29
24	22	30	27	

Challenge Your Thinking

The numbers in each row across total the numbers to the right of each row. The numbers in each column total the numbers at the bottom of each column.

Use numbers between 1 and 9 to fill in the spaces in the grid.

9	5	6	4	24
1	6	7	5	19
5	2	8	2	17
3	7	2	3	15
18	20	23	14	

Challenge Your Thinking

The numbers in each row across total the numbers to the right of each row. The numbers in each column total the numbers at the bottom of each column.

Use numbers between 1 and 10 to fill in the spaces in the grid.

5	7	5	6	23
5	6	10	8	29
8	5	9	4	26
3	7	8	7	25
21	25	32	25	

Challenge Your Thinking

The numbers in each row across total the numbers to the right of each row. The numbers in each column total the numbers at the bottom of each column.

Use numbers between 1 and 9 to fill in the spaces in the grid.

9	8	4	3	24
2	5	6	8	21
5	2	3	7	17
4	8	1	3	16
20	23	14	21	